Neon Broken Light

Lacie Grayson

BookLeaf Publishing

India | USA | UK

Presentation by *BookLeaf Publishing*

Web: www.bookleafpub.com

E-mail: info@bookleafpub.com

ISBN: 9789357214926

First edition 2022

To Charles David Taylor

ACKNOWLEDGEMENT

Aunt Leah, Teaching me to be myself even when people suck I miss you.
Grandma Lillian, Continue in peace. You were the reason my mom is insane but you were broken too. You gave me the stance of healing.

Cheryl, you are more in need of self awareness and forgiveness. But, you need to give that to you before anyone else can.

PREFACE

My dad wrote songs. I can also write songs. However, usually people just borrow lines I write. While we did lines off a mirror in a bathroom in NYC. Half of us hated admitting we lived in New Jersey.

I used to think it was enough to be there. But, as I'm getting older I'm realizing I want to be remembered for my own words.

My work.

Even for myself. To say I was here, I did the journey it was hard. Life is hard for hard for everyone. This was my struggle.

Voices

In the other room I heard talking.
My whole life. Talking. Sometimes
People were actually there.

Sometimes it was my stepdad telling my mom I
was a loser
I'd die alone or worse (to him) I'd live with them
forever

That to me was worse than actually dying.

I slept in my own dinning room in Detroit
So, I could see clients in my bedroom
I kept extensive toys and rubber clothes.

The ghosts reminded me. I was who I was.

Theirs.

The Blood Doll

2

To survive I became what I thought was beauty.
Untouchable, black haired sunshine.

Even though my skin was pale.
I knew, someday I'd either find my vampire, or
become one.

Tumblr-age

It became who were.
to try and build legend. A new god.
I was content watching the chaos.
I'd post my pictures, some art.
Having popcorn while
The Shane- Jeffree- Boneghazi bullshit
happened.
The indie sleaze, was just girls styling things
from bedrooms, pretending to we went to
parties.
Party girls then copied those looks.
It was one hell of a feedback loop
But, nothing quite like the days of t-shirt surgery
on livejournal.

That launched the internet's biggest scam artist.

Let Down

I knew I was a let down early on.
so life, to me was something to tested
to messed with.
I was a categorical disappoint. It never mattered
how nice I was. What I brought. Because of
things I can't control I'm never enough.

So,
I became so good at deify odds. Finding a
pattern and simply breaking it.
Some call it luck, its more defined patience.
Being told "Sit in the corner." "no one will want
you."

Someone
was listening

He didn't like it
  decided I was like him.
It took 39 years and so many crows.

Now, I know.

Love

5

a Western movie is a love story
 My mom is the type who chased men.
 I attract them. They become mine.
I believe love is just I was out gunned, or he
cheated and shot first.
I'd rather be an outlaw, ride through a town.
Attracting what comes.

Here I am gun-shy against the new boy.

He's an outlaw, a country boy with Lux Interior
vibe.
I'm standing here.

Swans

I know a secret.
Down by the lake.
I sit for hours. Debating my own wellness.
Sometimes I wonder if for the regal and royal.
 A Swans legs are just as frantic as a duck's
under the water. That says a lot about us, and
how we pretend things fine Never addressing
how hard it is.
But, I know.
The true secret.

Gia

Sometimes certain things stick with you.

Never more so for me than Gia.
 I watched it with Amber my childhood
bestfriend.
God knows her mother NEVER paid us any
mind.
 I think about Gia now.
How she's almost become a personal pantheon
 Her, Hunter Thompson, Sylvia Plath.
I don't know why.
Every so often a "Gia died for our sins" will post
come
and I'm at peace again.

Full Moon

sometimes O' the moon I find her captivating
I want to know the secrets of the universe
I find my mind escalating
My thoughts vacillate.
Between you my job, the old man and the sea
Does everyone chase something?
Never really getting anywhere?

Drip

Now, the kids the today say rizz.
and say it's like math for IF you could pull
A class D&D bard like myself charisma
But would never actually DO the math.
(we're too pretty)

what the hell do you think?

I want all the love and I'm not afraid to work.
You need to fear me first.
Because I'll pack a punch to your heart
you won't soon forget.

Drink Tickets

I got a mind to go out
 Tonight, it's my city
Tonight, its my time at the club.
Come on buy my ticket.
Ride my ride.
Come inside
Don't you want to?
I really want you too
I'm iconic for a reason, I don't live for drama.

Hello

Mama, I hate you less than you think
However you deserve it
You made everything a nightmare.
I get it

You had trauma but, I was eight its not fair.
I was a kid. I should've stayed a kid.
Refusing to stop.
Never truly giving up.
Sometimes the dream changes.
The message remains the same.

Crystal Duchess

I'm the I got a magic rock.
I'll give to you.
Because you look sad, or I love you.

(Maybe both I'll never tell)
I'm that iconic sardonic often classic lady
looking to heal
I've tried being quiet and endless pain, that didn't
seem to work
I don't have time for that sticky icky drama
That's reserved for my Mama.
My future family feels free express themselves
healing generational trauma.
I'm iconic for a reason, no matter the season.

Image

I wanted nothing. In my room.
Alone, I built up the excitement.
Waiting for the boom the applause.

I am clever in my endeavor.
I will not stop until I get what I want
Like a ghost to haunt.
I'll never stop pretending till it becomes real
I become what's in in my head

Vodka

Being totally honest it was never my drink, but whatever it was Friday night and I totally felt like getting bombed. I'm talking whole new levels of high score. They'd invent a new name for this.

Three Cherry Bombs (that's Rum and and Coke with a Grenadine shot followed by a swig of Rum Straight from the bottle, eat your heart out Johnny Depp) in and I was feeling it.
So, rather stupidly I switched to Vodka. Mostly, because it's what my best friend had. It seemed like a good idea. Never trust drunk thoughts.

Mine were typically dumb like "oh my god, I need the entire work of William S. Burroughs" Where as Elle's were strange like "oh my lets break out a Ouija board while we're all drunk." Yet, here I was in her house getting drunk. When some nameless male model type passed me a blunt.

I took a deep hit and considered my options. I
could bail now. Something in my swimming
head told me that was not happening.

"Peaches, do that thing you do." Elle asked me
begging in that way that gets her most things.
"It's not a thing." I say kind of trying to sink into
the sofa.
"It totally is. Just because one person hasn't
manifested right." Elle said sympathetically. I
knew she just wanted me to do what she wanted
but, it was nice hearing.

Session

Me: I feel all this pressure...but I don't think
anyone has loved me
Therapist: Why do feel this is happening?
Me: I find people who need something, so I
don't feel bad about asking for help.My adopted
mother, you know, the one who picked me?
-pauses sighs- she always made me ask for
things I needed. Like getting up in my
wheelchair? I COULD sit in front of it,it be five
minutes before the bus was coming.
She'd sit on the couch.

Therapist: People need to ask for help.

Me: -cutting her off- it was the way..she did it I'd
have to repeatedly ask, wait, sometimes my
needs would be putt off, things be worse for me.

Therapist: -calm- so, that's why you feel
impatient in your relationships now? And hate
repeating yourself or cycles..

Me: I mean it could be the reason, if that, I'm my
own best sadomasochist.

Smoke

Enraptured delight as I think about him.
Wondering why I'm like this?
He pulls on a cancer stick and I watch with
naked delight.
A smile forms we are in love with death and
beauty.

He blows the smoke in face and I swoon.
I fall in love a little more.

Guys in The City

In my twenties.
I was immensely used to putting in all the effort.
I convinced myself it turned me on to be forgot.
I'd throw a tantrum based absolute neglect.
Then do a cute apology.

Now, I've learnt.
State this is a need, tell my lover I may be a brat.
I am no longer prone to stupid fights.
I will not.
I can give a man everything. It has to beneficial,
or its not fair.

Let's cut to to the point.
Love should genuine care.
Beyond, what you feel in your pants
When I lived in NYC I couldn't tell the
difference.
It was my twenties, so I don't think it mattered
too much.

Really

All the lives I could choose.

Rockstar. Space Queen. Painter. Fashion
Designer.

Can I run them all in this life?
Can I be a hellhound?

May I be your guardian?
I can chase down everything for you.

I will bark at everything.
If you tell me I'm a good girl.
Make me a bed in hell on which we sleep.

Slime

Spinning lights. Pretty lights.
Illuminate even my dark and broken soul.
I can spin them
Like I spin your brain.
I want to break your brain
into pieces.

Like how I could trap you with kisses
when we younger.
I could tease you with a touch.
Your brain was and is mine.
It's as simple as knowing you
obsess over my breasts so
I wear red to highlight, necklaces.
I like to tease
you.

Being Dead On The Inside

When I feel something.
It feels better than nothing.

I usually feel nothing.

After years having my own heart broken.
By myself, men or my family.
I used to take feeling nothing as break.
After years of nothing.

I delight in something.

Even if its one sided, secret somethingness.

I Was Scared

As a kid.
I was scared. So many things, I blur together
now.
I can't remember certain parts.
So many "it didn't happen"

Make me question myself.

When I was a scared kid.